The Healing Power of Blake:
A Distillation

Edited and with an introduction by
John Diamond, M.D.

Publisher's Cataloging-in-Publication

Blake, William, 1757-1827.
    [Poems, Selections. 1998]
    The healing power of Blake: a distillation / edited
    and with an introduction by John Diamond. - -1st ed.
    p. cm.
    ISBN: 1-890995-03-7

    I. Diamond, John. II. Title.

PR4142.D53 1998   821'.7
                      QB198-1267

Published by Creativity Publishing, P.O. Box 544, Bloomingdale, IL 60108.

Printed by United Graphics, Mattoon, IL, on recycled paper using soy-based ink.

Cover photo by John Diamond

A Note on the Layout

*T*he greatest lines of Blake are long, too long for the average page.

The usual solutions have been to break the line, disturbing the flow and symmetry, or else to use a font so small that it reduces the significance of his utterance.

However, by turning the page, his lines can now be presented unimpeded, and as boldly as Blake deserves.

———

Preface

*F*or over thirty years, I have employed the therapeutic power of Poetry in my holistic practice, encouraging my patients to write their own poems, but also to read those of the masters: to read them aloud, and especially to sing them.

All creativity has the power to raise the Life Energy, the healing power within, the *vis medicatrix naturae* of Hippocrates. And poetry is no exception, in fact its ability is second only to that of music – and when it is sung it is, of course, the equal.

Over the years I have investigated and used many poems – at one time I had a library of over two thousand poetry books. I have researched many, many poems and have consistently, invariably, found those of Blake to have the greatest Healing Power. They are the most Therapeutic.

It is in this spirit that I offer you this selection of Blake at his most Life Energy enhancing. Not as a literary scholar, but as a doctor who respects, greatly, the supreme therapeutic value of High Creativity.

Blake may not, *per se*, heal the wound, but he will actuate the spirit. Of all the poets, he will most encourage your Will to be Well, your desire to gratefully embrace Life as passionately, as exuberantly, as exultantly, as he did.

For health, true Health, is the embracing of life in all of its vicissitudes, including its finality – the complete embracing – wholehearted, passionate, and blazingly intense.

It is the Heart-Knowledge of the Love, of the Belovedness Bestowed, and a joyous Song of Jubilation in grateful reciprocation. It is a life of fervent, zealous Enthusiasm. It is a life of love for the Love. Anything less than this is disease, a life of suffering. No one embraced Life more healthily than Blake.

No other poet, perhaps no other person, can through his writings, through his Self transmitted through his writings, so raise our Life Energy, the Healing Power within us – the aspiration to be fully Realized, to be truly Healthy.

For no other has so loved life, and so embraced it – and so surrendered it at his time.

And it is for this reason that for many years I have used him, more than all the other poets, however great, as an essential component of my healing practice.

In your hands you hold an essence of Blake's Existence, a eulogy to Life and Love.

Open your heart to him, as he did to you. Be suffused by his glory for Life, and embrace It.

Read him, now – aloud. Sing him, now – out loud as so many have done.

Feel your spirits lift, feel the Life Energy of Blake flowing through you – healing. This is the Power of the most Therapeutic of all the English poets.

This is the Healing Power of Blake.

A day will come when the Arts, especially Poetry and Music, will receive their true recognition and respect as being Great Therapies.

I believe that on that day Blake will be acclaimed as the first Master.

———

Introduction

Whenever I read from Blake's prophetic writings – anywhere – instantly I feel heat, burning heat, in the center of my chest: the blazing fire of love he ignites deep in my heart.

Often he seems unattractive, strange, even bizarre – sometimes incomprehensible. But, nonetheless, he fans and feeds my inner flame as no other poet has ever done.

I feel it now as I but think of reading him: under my breastbone – heat, burning heat. My heart aflame!

And this is but a lukewarm intimation of the passion, the blazing conflagration, that all but consumed Blake, and emanated from all his being as he etched – burned – his songs of Love Divine, his cantillations, onto the little copper plates. ("My fingers emit sparks of fire.")

From his depths the lava roars, louder than the furnaces of Los – and then explodes out onto the world, all molten, alive.

Yes, Blake, more than Yeats, really had a fire in his head. And the flames ever increased – I cannot imagine his red hair ever turning grey. Yes, fire in the head, and belly – and heart aflame. That's Blake!

And not to forget his visual art: no other poet has ever drawn the visions of which he writes with such clarity, such blinding intensity. There has never been such an artist, nor such a poet – let alone both as one!

Blake heard the Inner Voice more clearly than any poet, or composer. And he saw as keenly as Turner, perhaps even more so – and his stare was inward.

And he had the Power, fuelled by his fierce Desire, to precipitate it all into the outer world.

Shakespeare could retire, deserting, abandoning his Voice. Blake never! He listened ever more intently, and It sang with ever stronger Love, as did he in response. On his deathbed he sang exultantly, consumed by the flames of his final song.

Throughout time there have been but a few with such spiritual fire, with such burning outpourings of love for the Love. Certainly no other poet, or mystic, writing in English. Perhaps St. John of the Cross or another mystic from another land . . . perhaps only the Old Testament prophets.

But in English, only Blake – and only his prophetic writings, not the more formal poems, the ones we mostly know. They are generally younger, less mature, but that is not the reason.

Blake was saved by his anonymity. In his prophetic writings he is free – free of all the inhibitions and distortions of publication and performance. ("The outward Ceremony is Antichrist.") As he realized increasingly that few would ever see his works, they become ever more pure and true. They may be the purest poems we shall ever find, utterly unfettered by the chains of audience and publisher.

So was Hopkins – and he might have been almost another Blake had he not the need for a more structured religion. In this, too, Blake was free – completely. ("See Visions, Dream Dreams, and prophecy and speak Parables unobserv'd and at liberty from the Doubts of other mortals.")

This selection is therefore from Blake's prophetic works, although I have included a few excerpts from his other poems, and marginalia and letters. And, of course, there is Klopstock. I have taken many liberties with them, even versifying his prose or, more truthfully, his poetry presented as prose – for, even more than Dickens or Scott, Blake had no ordinary prose.

And I have punctuated him – in the ancient way: for the strongest vocal expression of the swelling power of his Pulsation.

My justification is my intent: for Blake to help you to open your heart – by feeling his love of Christ, God and Man.

I have chosen those passages which seem most accessible, complete, and intense – providing the best entry to his heart and soul. Not, at first, an easy man to understand – or to love. But the love is there, Oh, Yes! That particular, intensely personal, utterly idiosyncratic love that was Blake. That burning, blazing love.

And the passion – the Passion! Feel it! Let it sear your heart! and ignite your soul! Burn with Blake!

And don't just read them: Sing them – from your heart.

Sing! Exult! Jubilate! – like Blake!

———

The Healing Power of Blake

How I sang and call'd
the beasts and birds to their delights.

Thou hearest the Nightingale begin the Song of Spring;
The Lark sitting upon his earthy bed; just as the morn
Appears; listens silent; then springing from the waving Cornfield! loud
He leads the Choir of Day! trill, trill, trill, trill,
Mounting upon the wings of light into the Great Expanse:
Reecchoing against the lovely blue and shining heavenly Shell:
His little throat labours with inspiration, every feather
On throat and breast and wings vibrates with the effluence Divine.
All Nature listens silent to him, and the awful Sun
Stands still upon the Mountain, looking on this little Bird
With eyes of soft humility, and wonder, love and awe.
Then loud from their green covert, all the Birds begin their Song:
The Thrush, the Linnet and the Goldfinch, Robin and the Wren
Awake the Sun from his sweet reverie upon the Mountain:
The Nightingale again assays his song, and thro' the day,
And thro' the night warbles, luxuriant; every Bird of Song
Attending his loud harmony with admiration and love.

And the breath Divine is Love.

Then Mary burst forth into a Song! She flowed like a River of
Many Streams in the arms of Joseph and gave forth her tears of joy
Like many waters, and Emanating into gardens and palaces upon
Euphrates, and to forests and floods and animals wild and tame from
Gihon to Hiddekel, and to corn fields and villages and inhabitants
Upon Pison and Arnon and Jordan.

God Appears and God is Light
To those poor Souls who dwell in Night –
But does a Human Form Display
To those who Dwell in Realms of day.

In ignorance to view a small portion and think that All,
And call it Demonstration, blind to all the simple rules of life.

Man must,
and will,
have Some Religion.

She sat at the Mills, her hair unbound, her feet naked –
Cut with the flints: her tears run down: her reason grows like
The Wheel of Hand, incessant turning day and night without rest.
Insane, she raves upon the winds, hoarse, inarticulate.

Our own Imaginations –
those Worlds of Eternity
in which we shall live for ever.

Learn therefore, O Sisters, to distinguish the Eternal Human
That walks about among the stones of fire in bliss and woe
Alternate, from those States of Worlds in which the Spirit travels.
This is the only means to Forgiveness of Enemies.

Thro darkness deep
They bear the woven draperies: on golden hooks they hang abroad
The universal curtains, and spread out from Sun to Sun
The vehicles of light.

What is Mortality
But the things relating to the Body,
Which dies?
What is Immortality
But the things relating to the Spirit,
Which Lives Eternally?

Behold the time approaches fast, that thou shalt be as a thing
Forgotten – when one speaks of thee he will not be believ'd.
When the man gently fades away in his immortality –
When the mortal disappears in improved knowledge – cast away
The former things – so shall the Mortal gently fade away,
And so become invisible to those who still remain.

Listen, I will tell thee what is done in the caverns of the grave –
The Lamb of God has rent the Veil of Mystery soon to return
In Clouds and Fires around the rock and the Mysterious tree.
As the seed waits, Eagerly watching for its flower and fruit,
Anxious its little soul looks out into the clear expanse
To see if hungry winds are abroad with their invisible army,
So Man looks out in tree and herd and fish and bird and beast,
Collecting up the scatter'd portions of his immortal body
Into the Elemental forms of every thing that grows.
He tries the sullen north wind, riding on its angry furrows,
The sultry south when the sun rises – and the angry east
When the sun sets, when the clods harden and the cattle stand

Drooping, and the birds hide in their silent nests. He stores his thoughts
As in a store house, in his memory. He regulates the forms
Of all beneath and all above. And in the gentle West
Reposes, where the Sun's heat dwells. He rises to the Sun,
And to the Planets of the Night, and to the stars that gild
The Zodiac, and the stars that sullen stand to north and south.
He touches the remotest pole, and in the Center weeps
That Man should Labour, and sorrow, and learn and forget, and return
To the dark valley whence he came, to begin his labours anew.
In pain he sighs, in pain he labours in his universe,
Screaming in birds over the deep, and howling in the Wolf
Over the slain, and moaning in the cattle, and in the winds,
And weeping over Orc and Urizen. In clouds and flaming fires,
And in the cries of birth, and in the groans of death, his voice
Is heard throughout the Universe, wherever a grass grows
Or a leaf buds. The Eternal Man is seen, is heard. Is felt –
And all his Sorrows, till he reassumes his ancient bliss.

The idiot Reasoner laughs at the Man of Imagination:
And from laughter proceeds to murder by undervaluing calumny.

And every Generated Body in its inward form
Is a garden of delight and a building of magnificence.

I have innocence to defend, and ignorance to instruct.
I have no time for seeming, and little arts of compliment
In morality and virtue; in self-glorying and pride.

The open heart is shut up in integuments of frozen silence,
That the spear that lights it forth may shatter the ribs and bosom.

He who will not comingle in Love,
Must be adjoin'd by Hate.

The Lovers' night bears on my song,
And the nine Spheres rejoice beneath my powerful control –
They sing unceasing to the notes of my immortal hand.
The solemn silent moon
Reverberates the living harmony upon my limbs.
The birds and the beasts rejoice and play,
And every one seeks for his mate, to prove his inmost joy.

To bathe in the Waters of Life – to wash off the Not Human,
I come in Self-annihilation and the grandeur of Inspiration.
To cast off Rational Demonstration by Faith in the Saviour,
To cast off the rotten rags of Memory by Inspiration –
To cast off Bacon, Locke and Newton from Albion's covering,
To take off his filthy garments and clothe him with Imagination.
To cast aside from Poetry, all that is not Inspiration –
That it no longer shall dare to mock with the aspersion of Madness
Cast on the Inspired by the tame high finisher of paltry Blots,
Indefinite, or paltry Rhymes; or paltry Harmonies,
Who creeps into State Government like a catterpiller to destroy.
To cast off the idiot Questioner who is always questioning –
But never capable of answering; who sits with a sly grin
Silent plotting when to question – like a thief in a cave;
Who publishes doubt and calls it knowledge; whose Science is Despair,
Whose pretence to knowledge is Envy, whose whole Science is
To destroy the wisdom of ages to gratify ravenous Envy
That rages round him like a Wolf, day and night without rest.
He smiles with condescension; he talks of Benevolence and Virtue,
And those who act with Benevolence and Virtue, they murder time on time.

Do what you will, this Life's a Fiction,
And is made up of Contradiction.

In every bosom a Universe expands as wings.

He's a Blockhead who wants a proof of what he Can't Percieve –
And he's a Fool who tries to make such a Blockhead believe.

Go, tell them that the Worship of God is honouring his gifts
In other men, and loving the greatest men best, each according
To his Genius which is the Holy Ghost in Man.

And if he turned and view'd the unpass'd void,
upward was still his mighty wand'ring.

And if any enter into thee, thou shalt be an Unquenchable Fire.

Awake! awake O sleeper of the land of shadows – wake! expand!
I am in you and you in me, mutual in love divine:
Fibres of love from man to man thro' Albion's pleasant land.

He whose face gives no light, shall never become a star.

There is a Moment in each Day that Satan cannot find,
Nor can his Watch Fiends find it; but the Industrious find
This Moment and it multiply; and when it once is found
It renovates every Moment of the Day, if rightly placed.

Why stand we here trembling around
Calling on God for help,
And not ourselves, in whom God dwells,
Stretching a hand to save the falling Man?

Tell him to be no more dubious – demand explicit words.

Here are the stars created, and the seeds of all things planted;
And here the Sun and Moon receive their fixed destinations.

I took the sighs, and tears, and bitter groans.
I lifted them into my Furnaces
To form the spiritual sword
That lays open the hidden heart.

What is Sin but a little
Error and fault that is soon forgiven? but mercy is not a Sin,
Nor pity nor love nor kind forgiveness! O! if I have Sinned
Forgive and pity me! O! unfold thy Veil in mercy and love!

Let the Bulls of Luvah tread the Corn and draw the loaded waggon
Into the Barn while children glean the Ears around the door.
Then shall they lift their innocent hands and stroke his furious nose,
And he shall lick the little girl's white neck, and on her head
Scatter the perfume of his breath. While from his mountains high
The lion of terror shall come down, and bending his bright mane
And couching at their side, shall eat from the curl'd boy's white lap
His golden food; and in the evening sleep before the Door.

He who would see the Divinity, must see him in his Children.

Come hither, be patient. Let us converse together, because
I also tremble at myself and at all my former life.

Art is the Tree of Life.

Astonish'd, comforted, Delighted, in notes of Rapturous Extacy,
All Beulah stood astonish'd, Looking down to Eternal Death.
They saw the Savior beyond the Pit of death and destruction:
For whether they look'd upward they saw the Divine Vision,
Or whether they look'd downward still they saw the Divine Vision,
Surrounding them on all sides, beyond sin and death and hell.

Every human heart has
gates of brass
And bars of adamant
Which few dare unbar.

Improvement makes strait roads –
But the crooked roads without Improvement
Are roads of Genius.

Compell the poor to live upon a Crust of bread by soft mild arts –
Smile when they frown, frown when they smile; and when a man looks pale
With labour and abstinence, say he looks healthy and happy;
And when his children sicken, let them die – there are enough
Born, even too many, and our Earth will be overrun
Without these arts. If you would make the poor live with temper
With pomp give every crust of bread you give; with gracious cunning
Magnify small gifts; reduce the man to want a gift, and then give with pomp.
Say he smiles if you hear him sigh. If pale, say he is ruddy.
Preach temperance: say he is overgorg'd, and drowns his wit
In strong drink, tho' you know that bread and water are all
He can afford. Flatter his wife, pity his children, till we can
Reduce all to our will – as spaniels are taught with art.

Thy Clouds of Blessing, thy Cherubims of Tender-mercy
Stretching their Wings sublime over the Little-ones of Albion!

No man can think, write, or speak from his heart –
But he must intend truth.

In Great Eternity every particular Form gives forth or Emanates
Its own peculiar Light, and the Form is the Divine Vision,
And the Light is his Garment. This is Jerusalem in every Man,
A Tent and Tabernacle of Mutual Forgiveness, Male and Female Clothings.

Go therefore, cast out devils in Christ's name:
Heal thou the sick of spiritual disease.
Pity the evil, for thou art not sent
To smite with terror and with punishments
Those that are sick, like the Pharisees,
Crucifying and encompassing sea and land
For proselytes to tyranny and wrath;
But to the Publicans and Harlots go!
Teach them True Happiness, but let no curse
Go forth out of thy mouth to blight their peace –
For Hell is open'd to Heaven: thine eyes beheld
The dungeons burst and the Prisoners set free.

O search and see: turn your eyes upward: open, O thou World
Of Love and Harmony in Man. Expand thy ever lovely Gates!

She who adores not your frowns
will only loathe your smiles.

For all are Men in Eternity. Rivers, Mountains, Cities, Villages,
All are Human, and when you enter into their Bosoms you walk
In Heavens and Earths, as in your own Bosom you bear your Heaven
And Earth; and all you behold, tho' it appears Without, it is Within,
In your Imagination, of which this World of Mortality is but a Shadow.

And I became One Man with him arising in my strength.

Nine days she labour'd at her work – and nine dark sleepless nights.
But on the tenth trembling morn, the Circle of Destiny complete,
Round roll'd the sea – Englobing in a wat'ry Globe – self balanc'd.

Tho' thou art Worship'd by the Names Divine
Of Jesus and Jehovah, thou art still
The Son of Morn in weary Night's decline –
The lost Traveller's Dream under the Hill.

And she went forth and saw the forms of Life and of delight
Walking on Mountains, or flying in the open expanse of heaven.
She heard sweet voices in the winds, and in the voices of birds
That rose from waters.

Yet thou wast lovely as the summer cloud upon my hills
When Jerusalem was thy heart's desire, in times of youth and love.

Look! I have wept!
And given soft milk, mingled together with the spirits of flocks
Of lambs and doves, mingled together in cups and dishes
of painted clay.

And every Natural Effect has a Spiritual Cause,
And Not a Natural;
For a Natural Cause only seems:
It is a Delusion.

The noise of rural works resounded thro' the heavens of heavens.
The horses neigh from the battle. The wild bulls from the sultry waste,
The tygers from the forests, and the lions from the sandy desarts –
They sing. They sieze the instruments of harmony. They throw away
The spear, the bow, the gun, the mortar. They level the fortifications.

As when a man dreams, he reflects not that his body sleeps –
Else he would wake; so seem'd he entering his Shadow.

For every thing exists, and not one sigh nor smile nor tear,
One hair, nor particle of dust – not one – can pass away.

There is the Nettle that stings with soft down, and there
The indignant Thistle, whose bitterness is bred in his milk,
And who lives on the contempt of his neighbour: there all the idle weeds
That creep around the obscure places shew their various limbs,
Naked in all their beauty dancing round the Wine Presses.

Cities are Men, fathers of multitudes – and Rivers and Mountains
Are also Men. Every thing is Human, mighty! sublime!

Thy Bosom white, translucent, cover'd with immortal gems –
A sublime ornament not obscuring the outlines of beauty,
Terrible to behold for thy extreme beauty and perfection:
Twelve-fold here all the Tribes of Israel I behold.
Upon the Holy Land: I see the River of Life and Tree of Life.
I see the New Jerusalem descending out of Heaven,
Between thy Wings of gold and silver – feather'd, immortal,
Clear as the rainbow, as the cloud of the Sun's tabernacle.

Thy Reins, cover'd with Wings translucent, sometimes covering
And sometimes spread abroad, reveal the flames of holiness
Which, like a robe, covers, and like a Veil of Seraphim,
In flaming fire unceasing burns from Eternity to Eternity.

Twelvefold I there behold Israel in her Tents:
A Pillar of a Cloud by day, a Pillar of fire by night
Guides them; there I behold Moab and Ammon and Amalek.
There, Bells of silver round thy knees, living articulate
Comforting sounds of love and harmony, and on thy feet
Sandals of gold and pearl, and Egypt and Assyria before me.

Art and Science cannot exist, but by Naked Beauty displayd.

Make me not like the things forgotten, as they had not been.
Make me not, the thing that loveth thee, a tear wiped away.

The furious wind still rends around. They flee in sluggish effort.
They beg, they intreat in vain now – They Listen'd not to intreaty.
They view the flames red rolling on thro' the wide universe –
From the dark jaws of death beneath and desolate shores remote,
These covering vaults of heaven and these trembling globes of Earth.
One Planet calls to another and one star enquires of another
"What flames are these coming from the South? What noise, what dreadful rout –
As of a battle in the heavens? Hark! Heard you not the trumpet
As of fierce battle?" While they spoke the flames come on intense – roaring.

They see him whom they have pierc'd. They wail because of him.
They magnify themselves no more against Jerusalem, Nor
Against her little ones. The innocent accused before the Judges
Shines with immortal glory. Trembling, the Judge springs from his throne
Hiding his face in the dust beneath the prisoner's feet, and saying:
"Brother of Jesus, what have I done? Intreat thy lord for me –
Perhaps I may be forgiven." While he speaks the flames roll on,
And after the flame appears the Cloud of the Son of Man
Descending from Jerusalem with power and great Glory.
All nations look up to the Cloud and behold him who was Crucified.

A pretence of Art to destroy Art; a pretence of Liberty
To destroy Liberty; a pretence of Religion to destroy Religion.

O how can I with my gross tongue that cleaveth to the dust
Tell of the Four-fold man in starry numbers fitly order'd?
Or how can I with my cold hand of clay! But thou, O Lord,
Do with me as thou wilt! for I am nothing, and vanity.

For not one sparrow can suffer and the whole Universe not suffer also,
In all its Regions, and its Father and Saviour not pity and weep.

Loud! loud! the Mountains lifted up their voices! loud the Forests!
Rivers thunder'd against their banks, loud Winds furious fought.
Cities and Nations contended in fires and clouds and tempests!
The Seas raisd up their voices and lifted their hands on high!

Every Man's Wisdom is peculiar to his own Individuality.

O who would smile on the wintry seas
And Pity the stormy roar,
Or who will exchange his new born child
For the dog at the wintry door?

His bosom is like starry heaven expanded: all the stars
Sing round: there waves the harvest and the vintage rejoices; the Springs
Flow into rivers of delight; there the spontaneous flowers
Drink, laugh and sing, the grasshopper, the Emmet and the Fly;
The golden Moth builds there a house and spreads her silken bed.
His loins inwove with silken fires are like a furnace fierce –
As the strong Bull in summer time, when bees sing round the heath
Where the herds low after the shadow and after the water spring.
The num'rous flocks cover the mountain and shine along the valley.

The birds adore the sun, the beasts rise up and play in his beams;
And every flower and every leaf rejoices in his light.
Then, O thou fair one, sit thee down, for thou art as the grass:
Thou risest in the dew of morning and at night art folded up.

The Religions of all Nations are derived
from each Nation's different reception
Of the Poetic Genius.

Is not that Sun thy husband – and that Moon thy glimmering Veil?
Are not the Stars of heaven thy Children? Art thou not Babylon?
Art thou Nature, Mother of all? Is Jerusalem thy Daughter?

I know of no other Christianity –
And of no other Gospel –
Than the liberty, both of body and mind,
To exercise the Divine Arts of Imagination.

Man's desires are limited by his perceptions –
None can desire what he has not perciev'd.

She ceast,
And roll'd her shady clouds
Into the secret place.

Arise, you little glancing wings, and sing your infant joy!
Arise, and drink your bliss!
For every thing that lives is holy; for the source of life
Descends to be a weeping babe;
For the Earthworm renews the moisture of the sandy plain.

Poetry Fetter'd Fetters the Human Race!
Nations are Destroy'd or Flourish in proportion
As Their Poetry, Painting and Music are Destroy'd or Flourish!

And Now Begins a New life,
Because another covering of Earth
Is shaken off.

I am Inspired! I know it is Truth! for I Sing
According to the inspiration of the Poetic Genius
Who is the eternal all-protecting Divine Humanity
To whom be Glory and Power and Dominion Evermore.
Amen.

Thou percievest the Flowers put forth their precious Odours!
And none can tell how from so small a center comes such sweets,
Forgetting that within that Center Eternity expands
Its ever-during doors...
First eer the morning breaks, joy opens in the flowery bosoms –
Joy even to tears, which the Sun rising, dries: first the Wild Thyme
And Meadow-sweet, downy and soft, waving among the reeds
Light springing on the air, lead the sweet Dance – they wake
The Honeysuckle sleeping on the Oak; the flaunting beauty
Revels along upon the wind: the White-thorn lovely May
Opens her many lovely eyes, listening. The Rose still sleeps.
None dare to wake her. Soon she bursts her crimson curtain'd bed
And comes forth in the majesty of beauty; every Flower:
The Pink, the Jessamine, the Wall-flower, the Carnation
The Jonquil, the mild Lilly opes her heavens! Every Tree,
And Flower and Herb soon fill the air with an innumerable Dance –
Yet all in order sweet and lovely. Men are sick with Love!

What have I said? What have I done? O all-powerful Human Words!
You recoil back upon me in the blood of the Lamb slain in his Children.
Two bleeding Contraries, equally true, are his Witnesses against me.

To open the Eternal Worlds, to open the immortal Eyes
Of Man inwards into the Worlds of Thought, into Eternity
Ever expanding in the Bosom of God, the Human Imagination.

Why does the Raven cry aloud – and no eye pities her?
Why fall the Sparrow and the Robin in the foodless winter?
Faint! shivering, they sit on leafless bush or frozen stone,

Wearied with seeking food across the snowy waste, the little
heart cold, and the little tongue consum'd, that once in thoughtless joy
Gave songs of gratitude to waving cornfields round their nest.

Why howl the Lion and the Wolf – why do they roam abroad?
Deluded by summer's heat, they sport in enormous love,
And cast their young out to the hungry wilds and sandy desarts.

Why is the Sheep given to the knife? the Lamb plays in the Sun –
He starts! he hears the foot of Man! he says: Take thou my wool,
But spare my life: but he knows not that winter cometh fast.

The Spider sits in his labour'd Web – eager watching for the Fly.
Presently comes a famish'd Bird, and takes away the Spider.
His Web is left all desolate, that his little anxious heart
So careful wove, and spread it out with sighs and weariness.

Jesus died because he strove
Against the current of this Wheel. Its Name
Is Caiaphas, the dark Preacher of Death,
Of sin, of sorrow and of punishment:
Opposing Nature!

Knowledge is not by deduction,
But Immediate – by Perception or Sense
At once!

The Sun shall go before you in Day, the Moon shall go
Before you in Night. Come on! Come on! Come on! The Lord
Jehovah is before, behind, above, beneath, around.

That the Poetic Genius is the true Man,
And that the body, or outward form, of Man,
Is derived from the Poetic Genius.

Thus were the stars of heaven created like a golden chain,
To bind the body of Man to heaven – from falling into the Abyss.
Each took his station, and his course began with sorrow and care.
In sevens and ten and fifties, hundreds, thousands – number'd all
According to their various powers. Subordinate to Urizen
And to his sons in their degrees, and to his beauteous daughters,
Travelling in silent majesty along their order'd ways
In right lined paths outmeasur'd by proportions of number, weight,
And measure. Mathematic motion wondrous. Along the deep.
In fiery pyramid. Or Cube. Or unornamented pillar
Of fire far shining, travelling along, even to its destin'd end,
Then falling down. A terrible space. Recov'ring, in winter dire,
Its wasted strength, it back returns upon a nether course,
Till, fired with ardour fresh recruited in its humble season,
It rises up on high all summer, till its wearied course
Turn into autumn. Such the period of many worlds.
Others triangular, right angled course maintain. Others obtuse,
Acute, Scalene, in simple paths. But others move
In intricate ways biquadrate. Trapeziums. Rhombs, Rhomboids,
Paralellograms. Triple and quadruple. Polygonic
In their amazing, hard, subdued course in the vast deep.

What to others a trifle appears,
Fills me full of smiles, or tears.
For double the vision my Eyes do see
And a double vision is always with me:
With my inward Eye 'tis an old Man grey,
With my outward a Thistle across my way.

Wonder siez'd all in Eternity! to behold the Divine Vision open
The Center into an Expanse, and the Center rolled out into an Expanse.

Is that Calvary and Golgotha –
Becoming a building of pity and compassion? Lo!
The stones are pity, and the bricks well wrought affections,
Enamel'd with love and kindness – and the tiles engraven gold.
Labour of merciful hands: the beams and rafters are forgiveness:
The mortar and cement of the work, tears of honesty; the nails,
And the screws and iron braces, are well wrought blandishments,
And well contrived words, firm fixing, never forgotten,
Always comforting the remembrance: the floors, humility;
The ceilings, devotion; the hearths, thanksgiving.

Every Minute Particular is Holy.

I have tried to make friends by corporeal gifts but have only
Made enemies: I never made friends but by spiritual gifts.

The Spirit of Jesus is continual forgiveness of Sin:
He who waits to be righteous
Before he enters into the Saviour's kingdom, the Divine Body,
Will never enter there.

These the Visions of Eternity,
But we see only, as it were, the hem of their garments
When with our vegetable eyes we view these wond'rous Visions.

Thou'rt my Mother from the Womb,
Wife, Sister, Daughter, to the Tomb,
Weaving to Dreams the Sexual strife
And weeping over the Web of Life.

Still the faint harps and silver voices calm the weary couch,
But, from the caves of deepest night, ascending in clouds of mist,
The winter spread his wide black wings across from pole to pole:
Grim frost beneath and terrible snow, link'd in a marriage chain,
Began a dismal dance. The winds around on pointed rocks
Settled like bats innumerable, ready to fly abroad.

When Nations grow Old, The Arts grow Cold –
And Commerce settles on every Tree.

The books remain'd still unconsum'd,
Still to be written and interleav'd with brass and iron and gold,
Time after time – for such a journey none but iron pens
Can write, And adamantine leaves receive; nor can the man who goes
The journey obstinate refuse to write, time after time.

The Female searches sea and land for gratification to the
Male Genius, who in return clothes her in gems and gold,
And feeds her with the food of Eden – hence all her beauty beams.
She Creates at her will a little moony night, and silence,
With Spaces of sweet gardens, and a tent of elegant beauty:
Closed in by a sandy desart and a night of stars shining;
And a little tender moon and hovering angels on the wing.
And the Male gives a Time and Revolution to her Space,
Till the time of love is passed in ever varying delights.

Which way soever I turn – I behold Humanity and Pity!

Again he speaks in thunder, and in fire!
Thunder of Thought, flames of fierce desire:
Even from the depths of Hell his voice I hear
Within the unfathom'd caverns of my Ear.

We live as One Man; for, contracting our infinite senses,
We behold multitude, or expanding, we behold as one,
As One Man, all the Universal Family, and that One Man
We call Jesus the Christ; and he in us, and we in him
Live in perfect harmony in Eden, the land of life,
Giving, receiving, and forgiving each other's trespasses.

I gave sweet lillies to their breasts and roses to their hair.
I taught them songs of sweet delight. I gave their tender voices
Into the blue expanse, and I invented with laborious art
Sweet instruments of sound.

For thou art but a form and organ of life, and of thyself
Art nothing – being Created Continually by Mercy and Love divine.

Like a famish'd Eagle – Eyeless – raging in the vast exspanse;
Incessant tears are now my food, incessant rage and tears.

For All Things Exist in the Human Imagination.

Thou seest the Constellations in the deep and wondrous Night:
They rise in order and continue their immortal courses
Upon the mountains, and in vales, with harp and heavenly song,
With flute and clarion, with cups and measures fill'd with foaming wine.

There is no other God than that God
Who is the intellectual fountain of Humanity.

And the Bow is a Male and Female. And the Quiver of the Arrows of Love
Are the Children of this Bow, a Bow of Mercy and Loving kindness laying
Open the hidden Heart in Wars of mutual Benevolence, Wars of Love.

Prayer is the Study of Art,
Praise is the Practice of Art.

Both read the Bible day and night,
But thou read'st black where I read white.

Descend, O Lamb of God, and take away the imputation of Sin.

It is an easy thing to triumph in the summer's sun,
And in the vintage, and to sing on the waggon loaded with corn.
It is an easy thing to talk of patience to the afflicted,
To speak the laws of prudence to the houseless wanderer,
To listen to the hungry raven's cry in wintry season –
When the red blood is fill'd with wine, and with the marrow of lambs.

It is an easy thing to laugh at wrathful elements,
To hear the dog howl at the wintry door, the ox in the slaughter house moan;
To see a god on every wind and a blessing on every blast;
To hear sounds of love in the thunder storm that destroys our enemies' house;
To rejoice in the blight that covers his field,
and the sickness that cuts off his children –
While our olive and vine sing and laugh round our door
and our children bring fruits and flowers.

Then the groan and the dolor are quite forgotten, and the slave grinding at the mill,
And the captive in chains, and the poor in the prison; and the soldier in the field
When the shatter'd bone hath laid him groaning among the happier dead.
It is an easy thing to rejoice in the tents of prosperity –
Thus could I sing and thus rejoice, but it is not so with me!

When on the highest lift of his light pinions, he arrives
At that bright Gate, another Lark meets him, and back to back
They touch their pinions, tip tip, and each descend
To their respective Earths; and there all night consult with Angels
Of Providence and with the Eyes of God – all night in slumbers
Inspired, and at the dawn of day send out another Lark
Into another Heaven to carry news upon his wings.

In my Brain are studies and Chambers
Filld with books and pictures of old
Which I wrote and painted in ages of Eternity,
Before my mortal life,
And whose works are the delight and Study of Archangels.
Why then should I be anxious
About the riches or fame of mortality.

Sure thou art bath'd in rivers of delight, on verdant fields
Walking in joy; in bright Expanses sleeping on bright clouds.

Thou art one with her, and knowest not of self in thy supreme joy.

If you account it Wisdom when you are angry, to be silent and
Not to shew it; I do not account that Wisdom, but Folly.

General Forms have their vitality in Particulars –
And every Particular is a Man,
A Divine Member of the Divine Jesus.

The feast was spread in the bright South, and the Regenerate Man
Sat at the feast rejoicing; and the wine of Eternity
Was serv'd round by the flames of Luvah all Day and all the Night.

I cry Love! Love! Love!
Happy, happy Love!
Free as the mountain wind!

O what is Life and what is Man. O what is Death? Wherefore
Are you my Children, natives in the Grave to where I go,
Or are you born to feed the hungry ravenings of Destruction,
To be the sport of Accident! To waste in Wrath and Love, a weary
Life, in brooding cares and anxious labours, that prove but chaff.

O I am nothing when I enter into judgment with thee.
If thou withdraw thy breath, I die and vanish into Hades.
If thou dost lay thine hand upon me, behold I am silent.
If thou withhold thine hand, I perish like a fallen leaf.
O I am nothing – and to nothing must return again.
If thou withdraw thy breath, behold I am oblivion.

Singular and Particular Detail
Is the Foundation of the Sublime.

As all men are alike (tho' infinitely various),
So all Religions and, as all similars, have one source.
The true Man is the source, he being the Poetic Genius.

God out of Christ is a Consuming Fire.

The Sun arises from his dewy bed, and the fresh airs
Play in his smiling beams giving, the seeds of life to grow.
And the fresh Earth beams forth ten thousand thousand springs of life.

Everything in Eternity
is transluscent.

Christ took on Sin in the Virgin's Womb and put it off on the Cross.

In Beulah the Female lets down her beautiful Tabernacle,
Which the Male enters magnificent between her Cherubim
And becomes One with her, mingling, condensing in Self-love.

These nostrils that expanded with delight in morning skies
I have bent downward with lead melted in my roaring furnaces
Of affliction, of love, of sweet despair, of torment unendurable.
My soul is seven furnaces; incessant roars the bellows
Upon my terribly flaming heart, the molten metal runs
In channels thro' my fiery limbs. O love, O pity, O fear,
O pain! O the pangs, the bitter pangs of love forsaken!

He who binds to himself a joy
Does the winged life destroy:
But he who kisses the joy as it flies
Lives in eternity's sun rise.

God becomes as we are – that we may be as he is.

Reason says 'Miracle' – Newton says 'Doubt'.
Aye! that's the way to make all Nature out.
'Doubt, Doubt, and don't believe without experiment':
That is the very thing that Jesus meant
When he said, 'Only Believe! Believe and try!
Try, Try, and never mind the Reason why.'

I wake sweet joy in dens of sorrow,
And I plant a smile
In forests of affliction –
And wake the bubbling springs of life,
In regions of dark death.

If I were pure, never could I taste the sweets
Of the Forgiveness of Sins. If I were holy, I never could behold the tears
Of love of him who loves me in the midst of his anger in furnace of fire.

Can a Poet doubt the Visions of Jehovah?
Nature has no Outline, but Imagination has.
Nature has no Tune, but Imagination has!
Nature has no Supernatural and dissolves:
Imagination is Eternity.

I am in God's presence night and day –
And he never turns his face away.

And every Moment has a Couch of gold for soft repose –
(A Moment equals a pulsation of the artery) –
And between every two Moments stands a Daughter of Beulah,
To feed the Sleepers on their Couches with maternal care.
And every Minute has an azure Tent, with silken Veils.
And every Hour has a bright golden Gate, carved with skill.
And every Day and Night has Walls of brass, and Gates of adamant,
Shining like precious Stones, and ornamented with appropriate signs:
And every Month, a silver paved Terrace builded high:
And every Year, invulnerable Barriers with high Towers:
And every Age is Moated deep with Bridges of silver and gold.
And every Seven Ages is Incircled with a Flaming Fire.
Now, Seven Ages is amounting to Two Hundred Years.
Each has its Guard, each Moment, Minute, Hour, Day, Month and Year.
All are the work of Fairy hands of the Four Elements:
The Guard are Angels of Providence on duty evermore.
Every Time less than a pulsation of the artery
Is equal, in its period and value, to Six Thousand Years.
For in this Period the Poet's Work is Done: and all the Great
Events of Time start forth and are conciev'd in such a Period –
Within a Moment: a Pulsation of the Artery.

That Man may be purified by the death of thy delusions.

Can Wisdom be put in a silver rod,
Or Love in a golden bowl?

There is no Limit of Expansion!
There is no Limit of Translucence
In the bosom of Man for ever
From eternity to eternity.

Vengeance is the destroyer of Grace
and Repentance in the bosom
of the Injurer, in which the Divine Lamb is cruelly slain.

Every honest man is a Prophet.

The Vegetative Universe opens like a flower from the Earth's center,
In which is Eternity. It expands in Stars to the Mundane Shell,
And there it meets Eternity again, both within and without.

I have been very near the Gates of Death
And have returned very weak
And an Old Man feeble and tottering,
But not in Spirit and Life –
Not in The Real Man –
The Imagination which Liveth for Ever.
In that I am stronger and stronger
As this Foolish Body decays.

We are not Individuals but States: Combinations of Individuals.

Each in his station,
Fixt in the Firmament,
By Peace, Brotherhood and Love.

The nature of infinity is this: That every thing has its
Own Vortex; and when once a traveller thro' Eternity
Has pass'd that Vortex, he percieves it roll backward behind
His path, into a globe itself infolding; like a sun:
Or like a moon, or like a universe of starry majesty,
While he keeps onwards in his wondrous journey on the earth;
Or like a human form – a friend with whom he liv'd benevolent.
As the eye of man views both the east and west, encompassing
Its vortex; and the north and south, with all their starry host;
Also the rising sun and setting moon he views surrounding
His corn-fields and his valleys of five hundred acres square.
Thus is the earth one infinite plane, and not as apparent
To the weak traveller, confin'd beneath the moony shade.
Thus is the heaven a vortex pass'd already, and the earth
A vortex, not yet pass'd by the traveller thro' Eternity.

And on the river's margin she ungirded her golden girdle:
She stood in the river and view'd herself within the wat'ry glass,
And her bright hair was wet with the waters. She rose up from the river,
And as she rose her Eyes were open'd to the world of waters.

There is a Void, outside of Existence,
Which, if enter'd into,
Englobes itself and becomes a Womb.

And Throughout all Eternity
I forgive you – you forgive me.
As our dear Redeemer said:
'This the Wine, and this the Bread.'

Awake, awake, thou child of dewy tears!
Open the orbs of thy blue eyes, and smile upon my gardens.

How do you know but ev'ry Bird that cuts the airy way,
Is an immense world of delight, clos'd by your senses five?

I carried her in my bosom, as a man carries a lamb.
I loved her, I gave her all my soul and my delight.
I hid her in soft gardens and in secret bowers of Summer,
Weaving mazes of delight along the sunny Paradise –
Inextricable labyrinths. She bore me sons and daughters.

Man fell upon his face prostrate before the wat'ry shadow,
Saying, 'O Lord, whence is this change? thou knowest I am nothing.'

There is in Eden a sweet River of mild and liquid pearl.

All deities reside in the human breast.

Come to my arms and never more
Depart, but dwell for ever here:
Create my Spirit to thy Love:
Subdue my Spectre to thy Fear.

The Eternal Promise
They wrote on all their tombs and pillars, and on every Urn
These words: 'If ye will believe, your Brother shall rise again,'
In golden letters ornamented with sweet labours of Love,
Waiting with Patience for the fulfilment of the Promise Divine.

We who dwell on Earth can do nothing of ourselves:
Every thing is conducted by Spirits, no less than Digestion or Sleep.

For her delight the horse his proud neck bow'd and his white mane,
And the Strong Lion deign'd in his mouth to wear the golden bit –
While the far beaming Peacock waited on the fragrant wind
To bring her fruits of sweet delight from trees of richest wonders,
And the strong pinion'd Eagle bore the fire of heaven in the night season.

Purple night, and crimson morning and golden day, descending
Thro' the clear changing atmosphere, display'd green fields among
The varying clouds, like paradises stretch'd in the expanse,
With towns and villages and temples, tents, sheepfolds and pastures,
Where dwell the children of the elemental worlds in harmony.

Why should Punishment Weave the Veil with Iron Wheels of War
When Forgiveness might it Weave with Wings of Cherubim?

The nature of a Female Space is this: it shrinks the Organs
Of Life till they become Finite and Itself seems Infinite.

To my Friend Butts I write
My first Vision of Light,
On the yellow sands sitting:
The Sun was Emitting
His Glorious beams
From Heavens high Streams.
Over Sea over Land
My Eyes did Expand
Into regions of air
Away from all Care,
Into regions of fire
Remote from Desire.
The Light of the Morning,
Heavens Mountains adorning,
In particles bright
The jewels of Light
Distinct shone and clear –
Amaz'd and in fear,
I each particle gazed,
Astonish'd, Amazed,

For each was a Man
Human form'd. Swift I ran
For they beckon'd to me
Remote by the Sea
Saying: Each grain of Sand,
Every Stone on the Land,
Each rock and each hill,
Each fountain and rill,
Each herb and each tree,
Mountain, hill, Earth and Sea,
Cloud, Meteor and Star
Are Men Seen Afar.
I stood in the Streams
Of Heaven's bright beams
And Saw Felpham sweet
Beneath my bright feet
In soft Female charms.
And in her fair arms
My shadow I knew –
And my wife's shadow too,

And My Sister and Friend
We like Infants descend
In our Shadows on Earth,
Like a weak mortal birth.
My Eyes more and more,
Like a Sea without shore,
Continue Expanding,
The Heavens commanding,
Till the Jewels of Light,
Heavenly Men beaming bright,
Appear'd as One Man
Who Complacent began
My limbs to infold
In his beams of bright gold.
Like dross, purg'd away
All my mire and my clay,
Soft consum'd in delight
In his bosom sun bright
I remain'd. Soft he smil'd
And I heard his voice Mild

Saying This is My Fold
O thou Ram horn'd with gold
Who awakest from sleep
On the sides of the Deep.
On the Mountains around
The roarings resound
Of the lion and wolf,
The loud sea and deep gulf:
These are guards of My Fold,
O thou Ram horn'd with gold!
And the voice faded mild –
I remain'd as a Child.
All I ever had known
Before me bright Shone.
I saw you and your wife
By the fountains of Life.
Such the Vision to me
Appear'd on the Sea.

The Infinite alone resides in Definite and Determinate Identity.

Where is the voice of God that call'd me from the silent dew?

This world of Imagination is the World of Eternity:
It is the Divine bosom into which we shall all go
After the death of the Vegetated body.
This World of Imagination is Infinite and Eternal,
Whereas the world of Generation or Vegetation
Is Finite and Temporal.
There Exists in that Eternal World
The Permanent Realities of Every Thing
Which we see reflected
In this Vegetable Glass of Nature.

Beneath the bottoms of the Graves which is Earth's central joint
There is a place where Contrarieties are equally true.
From this sweet Place Maternal Love awoke Jerusalem.
With pangs she forsook Beulah's pleasant lovely shadowy Universe
Where no dispute can come, created for those who Sleep.

I must Create a System – or be enslav'd by another Man's.
I will not Reason and Compare: my business is to Create.

Now Man was come to the Palm tree, and to the Oak of Weeping
Which stand upon the Edge of Beulah; and he sunk down
From the Supporting arms of the Eternal Saviour who dispos'd
The pale limbs of his Eternal Individuality
Upon The Rock of Ages, Watching over him with Love and Care.

There is from Great Eternity a mild and pleasant rest
Nam'd Beulah, a Soft Moony Universe, feminine, lovely:
Pure, mild and Gentle, given in Mercy to those who sleep,
Eternally Created by the Lamb of God, around,
On all sides, within and without the Universal Man.
The Daughters of Beulah follow sleepers in all their Dreams
Creating Spaces, lest they fall into Eternal Death.
The Circle of Destiny complete, they gave to it a Space
And nam'd the Space Ulro, and brooded over it in care and love.

He who has few Things to desire
cannot have many to fear.

In my bosom is milk and wine –
And a fountain from my breast.

Every word and every letter is studied and put into its fit place;
The terrific numbers are reserved for the terrific parts,
The mild and gentle for the mild and gentle parts,
And the prosaic for inferior parts;
All are necessary to each other.

And the Divine hand was upon them, bearing them thro' darkness
Back safe to their Humanity – as doves to their windows.

Man liveth not by Self alone, but in his brother's face
Each shall behold the Eternal Father and love and joy abound.

Sweet Mercy leads me on,
With soft repentant moan
I see the break of day.

The ocean calm, the clouds fold round – and fiery flames of love
Inwrap the immortal limbs; struggling in terrific joy.

My Garments shall be woven of sighs, and heart-broken lamentations.
The misery of unhappy Families shall be drawn out into its border,
Wrought with the needle with dire sufferings, poverty, pain, and woe,
Along the rocky Island and thence throughout the whole Earth.

For every thing that lives is holy.

Then Man ascended mourning into the splendors of his palace.
Above him rose a Shadow, from his wearied intellect
Of living gold – pure, perfect, holy: in white linen pure he hover'd,
A sweet entrancing self delusion, a wat'ry vision of Man
Soft exulting in existence, all the Man absorbing.

In Selfhood we are nothing – but fade away in morning's breath.

The Male is a Furnace of beryll;
The Female is a golden Loom.

He who will not defend Truth, may be compelled to
Defend a Lie, that he may be snared and caught and taken.

Where shall we take our stand to view the infinite and unbounded?

The Divine Vision became First a burning flame, then a column
Of fire, then an awful fiery wheel surrounding earth and heaven.

He who sees the Infinite in all things, sees God.
He who sees Ratio only, sees himself only.

I walk among his flocks and hear the bleating of his lambs:
O that I could behold his face and follow his pure feet –
I walk by the footsteps of his flocks. Come hither, tender flocks,
Can you converse with a pure Soul that seeketh for her maker?
You answer not: then am I set your mistress in this garden.
I'll watch you and attend your footsteps. You are not like the birds
That sing and fly in the bright air – but you do lick my feet,
And let me touch your wooly backs. Follow me as I sing,
For in my bosom a new song arises to my Lord:

Rise up, O sun, most glorious minister and light of day.
Flow on, ye gentle airs, and bear the voice of my rejoicing –
Wave freshly, clear water flowing around the tender grass,
And thou, sweet smelling ground, put forth thy life in fruits and flowers.
Follow me, O my flocks, and hear me sing my rapturous Song:
I will cause my voice to be heard on the clouds that glitter in the sun.
I will call; and who shall answer me? I will sing, who shall reply?
For from my pleasant hills behold the living, living springs

Running among my green pastures – delighting among my trees.
I am not here alone: my flocks, you are my brethren –
And you birds that sing and adorn the sky, you are my sisters.
I sing, and you reply to my Song. I rejoice, and you are glad.
Follow me, O my flocks: we will now descend into the valley.
O how delicious are the grapes flourishing in the Sun!
How clear the spring of the rock, running among the golden sand!
How cool the breezes of the valley! And the arms of the branchy trees
Cover us from the Sun! come and let us sit in the Shade.
My Luvah here hath plac'd me, in a Sweet and pleasant Land,
And given me fruits and pleasant waters, and warm hills and cool valleys.
Here will I build myself a house, and here I'll call on his name.
Here I'll return when I am weary and take my pleasant rest.

So spoke the Sinless Soul, and laid her head on the downy fleece
Of a curl'd Ram who stretch'd himself in sleep beside his mistress.
And soft sleep fell upon her eyelids in the silent noon of day.

If the Sun and Moon should Doubt,
They'd immediately Go out.

Repose on me till the morning of the Grave. I am thy life.

Terror struck in the Vale. I stood at that immortal sound:
My bones trembled. I fell outstretch'd upon the path
A moment, and my Soul return'd into its mortal state –
To Resurrection and Judgment in the Vegetable Body.
And my sweet Shadow of Delight stood trembling by my side.

The Imagination is not a State – it is the Human Existence itself.
Affection or Love becomes a State when divided from Imagination.
The Memory is a State always, and the Reason is a State
Created to be Annihilated and a new Ratio Created.
Whatever can be Created can be Annihilated – Forms cannot.
The Oak is cut down by the Ax, the Lamb falls by the Knife,
But their Forms Eternal Exist For-ever. Amen. Hallelujah!

Sometimes I curse – and sometimes bless – thy fascinating beauty.
Once Man was occupied in intellectual pleasures and energies,
But now my soul is harrow'd with grief and fear, and love and desire,
And now I hate and now I love, and Intellect is no more:
There is no time for any thing but the torments of love and desire.

Attempting to be more than Man –
We become less.

He became what he was doing – he was himself transform'd.

I am perhaps the most sinful of men:
I pretend not to holiness,
yet I pretend to love, to see,
To converse with daily as man with man,
And the more to have an interest in the Friend of Sinners.

Innocence dwells with Wisdom – but never with Ignorance.

I turn my eyes to the Schools and Universities of Europe
And there behold the Loom of Locke, whose Woof rages dire,
Wash'd by the Water-wheels of Newton. Black the cloth –
In heavy wreathes – folds over every Nation: cruel Works
Of many Wheels I view, wheel without wheel, with cogs tyrannic,
Moving by compulsion each other: not as those in Eden: which,
Wheel within Wheel, in freedom revolve in harmony and peace.

Let him not say that he knows better than his master –
For he only holds a candle in sunshine.

And they conversed together in Visionary forms dramatic which bright
Redounded from their Tongues in thunderous majesty, in Visions,
In new Expanses, creating exemplars of Memory and of Intellect,
Creating Space. Creating Time, according to the wonders Divine
Of Human Imagination throughout all the Three Regions immense
Of Childhood, Manhood and Old Age.

If the doors of perception were cleansed,
Every thing would appear to man as it is,
Infinite:
For man has closed himself up,
Till he sees all things thro' narrow chinks
Of his cavern.

Doth the voice of my Lord call me again? Am I pure thro' his Mercy
And Pity? Am I become lovely as a Virgin in his sight, who am
Indeed a Harlot drunken with the Sacrifice of Idols? Does he
Call her pure as he did in the days of her Infancy when She
Was cast out to the loathing of her person? The Chaldean took
Me from my Cradle. The Amalekite stole me away upon his Camels
Before I had ever beheld with love the Face of Jehovah, or known
That there was a God of Mercy. O Mercy, O Divine Humanity!
O Forgiveness and Pity and Compassion! If I were Pure I should never
Have known Thee; If I were Unpolluted I should never have
Glorified thy Holiness or rejoiced in thy great Salvation.

There is a God of This World.
A God Worship'd in this World as God;
And Set above all that is call'd God.

Follow with me my Plow.

The midst between: an Equilibrium grey, of air serene,
Where he might live in peace and where his life might meet repose.

Thou seest the Sun in heavy clouds
Struggling to rise above the Mountains, in his burning hand
He takes his Bow, then chooses out his arrows of flaming gold.
Murmuring, the Bowstring breathes with ardor!

As in Climes of happy Eternity
Where the lamb replies to the infant voice and the lion to the man of years,
Giving them sweet instructions; Where the Cloud, the River and the Field
Talk with the husbandman and shepherd.

The ever pitying one who seeth all things saw his fall,
And in the dark vacuity created a bosom of clay.

I hear a voice you cannot hear that says I must not stay:
I see a hand you cannot see that beckons me away.

All Distress inflicted by Heaven is a Mercy.

If it were not for the Poetic or Prophetic character,
The Philosophic and Experimental would soon be at the ratio of all things,
And stand still,
Unable to do other than repeat the same dull round over again.

Come, O thou Lamb of God, and take away the remembrance of Sin.
To Sin, and to hide the Sin in sweet deceit, is lovely!!
To Sin in the open face of day is cruel and pitiless! But
To record the Sin for a reproach – to let the Sun go down
In a remembrance of the Sin – is a Woe and a Horror!
A brooder of an Evil Day, and a Sun rising in blood.
Come then, O Lamb of God, and take away the remembrance of Sin.

There is a Grain of Sand in Lambeth that Satan cannot find,
Nor can his Watch Fiends find it: 'tis translucent and has many Angles,
But he who finds it will find Oothoon's palace: for within,
Opening into Beulah, every angle is a lovely heaven.

For every Pleasure Money Is Useless.

What is the price of Experience? do men buy it for a song?
Or wisdom for a dance in the street? No, it is bought with the price
Of all that a man hath – his house, his wife, his children.
Wisdom is sold in the desolate market where none come to buy,
And in the wither'd field where the farmer plows for bread in vain.

The Daughters of beauty look up from their Loom and prepare
The integument soft for its clothing with joy and delight.

The Divine Vision still was seen.
Still was the Human Form Divine,
Weeping in weak and mortal clay.
O Jesus, still the Form was thine.
And thine the Human Face, and thine
The Human Hands and Feet and Breath,
Entering thro' the Gates of Birth –
And passing thro' the Gates of Death.
And O thou Lamb of God, whom I
Slew in my dark self-righteous pride,
Art thou return'd to Albion's Land?
And is Jerusalem thy Bride?

The living voice is ever living in its inmost joy.

When Klopstock England defied,
Uprose terrible Blake in his pride –
For old Nobodaddy aloft
Farted and Belch'd and cough'd;
Then swore a great oath that made heav'n quake,
And call'd aloud to English Blake.
Blake was giving his body ease
At Lambeth beneath the poplar trees.
From his seat then started he,
And turn'd himself round three times three.
The Moon at that sight blush'd scarlet red,
The stars threw down their cups and fled,
And all the devils that were in hell
Answered with a ninefold yell.
Klopstock felt the intripled turn,
And all his bowels began to churn,
And his bowels turned round three times three
And lock'd in his soul with a ninefold key,
That from his body it ne'er could be parted
Till to the last trumpet it was farted.

Then again old nobodaddy swore
He ne'er had seen such a thing before –
Since Noah was shut in the ark,
Since Eve first chose her hell fire spark,
Since 'twas the fashion to go naked –
Since the old anything was created.
And in pity, he beg'd him to turn again
And ease poor Klopstock's nine fold pain.
From pity then he redend round –
And the ninefold Spell unwound.
If Blake could do this when he rose up from shite,
What might he not do if he sat down to write?

What is the Joy of Heaven
But Improvement in the things of the Spirit?

Glory! Glory! Glory! to the Holy Lamb of God.
I touch the heavens, as an instrument to glorify the Lord!

Man cannot know what passes in his members,
Till periods of Space and Time
Reveal the secrets of Eternity.

O Saviour pour upon me thy Spirit of meekness and love!
Annihilate the Selfhood in me: be thou all my life!

I give you the end of a golden string –
Only wind it into a ball:
It will lead you in at Heaven's gate
Built in Jerusalem's wall.

Man has no Body distinct from his Soul,
For that call'd Body is a portion of Soul
discern'd by the five Senses –
The chief inlets of Soul in this age.

O why was I born with a different face,
Why was I not born like the rest of my race?
When I look each one starts! when I speak I offend –
Then I'm silent and passive and lose every Friend.

Then my verse I dishonour. My pictures despise.
My person degrade and my temper chastise.
And the pen is my terror. The pencil my shame:
All my Talents I bury, and Dead is my Fame.

I am either too low or too highly priz'd –
When Elate I am Envy'd, When Meek I'm despis'd.

And I will lead thee thro' the Wilderness in shadow of my cloud,
And in my love I will lead thee, lovely Shadow of Sleeping Albion.

All Human Forms identified, even Tree, Metal, Earth and Stone: all
Human forms identified, living, going forth and returning wearied
Into the Planetary lives of Years, Months, Days and Hours: reposing,
And then Awaking into his Bosom in the Love of Immortality.

He who would do good to another must do it in Minute Particulars –
General Good is the plea of the scoundrel, hypocrite and flatterer.

The Human Imagination –
Which is the Divine Vision and Fruition
In which Man liveth eternally.

And every Space that a Man views around his dwelling-place,
Standing on his own roof, or in his garden on a mount
Of twenty-five cubits in height, such space is his Universe;
And on its verge the Sun rises and sets. The Clouds bow
To meet the flat Earth and the Sea in such an order'd Space:
The Starry heavens reach no further, but here bend and set
On all sides, and the two Poles turn on their valves of gold:
And if he move his dwelling-place, his heavens also move.
Where'er he goes. And all his neighbourhood bewail his loss:
Such are the Spaces called Earth, and such its dimension.

Trembling she wept over the Space, and clos'd it with a tender Moon.

*O*n the day of his death he stopped work and turned to Catherine, who was in tears; 'Stay, Kate!' he said, 'keep just as you are – I will draw your portrait – for you have ever been an angel to me.'

When he had completed it he put it down, and then began to sing verses and hymns. 'My beloved, they are not mine,' he told his wife as she listened to what she later called songs of joy and Triumph. 'No – they are not mine .' He was singing out of gladness.

It is written that "He died on Sunday night at 6 o'clock in a most glorious manner. Just before he died His Countenance became fair. His eyes Brighten'd and He burst out into Singing of the things he saw in Heaven".

———

The purpose of poetry is to give us an intimation of the Spirit.

And no poet ever did this more than Blake.

This is his greatest gift.

*T*he editor of this selection is not an academician, nor a poet, but a particular medical doctor. One who has transcended the medical model, concentrating not on the negative, the disease, but on the positive – the sufferer's innate healing power, his spirit, his Life Energy. For it is only this that can bring about not the mere alleviation of symptoms but the true cure.

An essential component of his practice is the encouragement of Creativity, to help the sufferer make the best choices for life and love, using poetry as a metaphor. Blake is a glorious example.

And to help the sufferer to feel the Pulse of life, to accept it, to surrender to it. And the pulse of Blake's poetry is the closest of all to the Pulse, to the Way.

———

Books by Dr. John Diamond:

Your Body Doesn't Lie
Life Energy: Unlocking the Hidden Power of Your Emotions to Achieve Total Well-Being
Life-Energy Analysis: A Way to Cantillation
The Re-Mothering Experience: How to Totally Love
The Life Energy in Music (The Life Energy in Music, Volume I)
The Wellspring of Music (The Life Energy in Music, Volume II)
The Heart of Music (The Life Energy in Music, Volume III)
A Spiritual Basis of Holistic Therapy
The Collected Papers, Volumes I and II
Speech, Language and the Power of the Breath
A Book of Cantillatory Poems
A Prayer On Entering: The Healer's Hearth a Sanctuary
Drumming with Spirit: The Way of the Pulse (late 1998)

All books available from: The Diamond Center
P. O. Box 381
South Salem, New York 10590
USA